Charles Plowden

A Short Account of the Establishment of the New See of

Baltimore in Maryland

Charles Plowden

A Short Account of the Establishment of the New See of Baltimore in Maryland

ISBN/EAN: 9783337817008

Printed in Europe, USA, Canada, Australia, Japan

Cover: Foto ©Suzi / pixelio.de

More available books at **www.hansebooks.com**

AN ACCOUNT

OF THE

CONSECRATION,

BY ONE BISHOP,

A BISHOP "IN PARTIBUS,"

OF THE

FIRST ROMISH BISHOP

IN THE

UNITED STATES.

1 REPRINT, BY PHOTO-LITHOGRAPHIC PROCESS, OF
A CONTEMPORANEOUS ROMISH PAMPHLET.

✠

NEW YORK:
REPRINTED IN FAC-SIMILE FOR THE HISTORICAL CLUB.
MDCCCLXXVI.

A SHORT ACCOUNT

OF THE

ESTABLISHMENT

OF THE

New See of Baltimore in Maryland,

AND OF CONSECRATING THE

Right Rev. Dr. JOHN CARROLL firſt BISHOP thereof

On the Feaſt of the Aſſumption, 1790.

WITH A

DISCOURSE

DELIVERED ON THAT OCCASION,

AND THE AUTHORITY FOR CONSECRATING THE
BISHOP, AND ERECTING AND ADMINISTERING
THE SAID SEE.

TO WHICH ARE ADDED

EXTRACTS from the different BILLS of RIGHT and
CONSTITUTION of the UNITED STATES,—That
Liberty of Conſcience is the Birth-right of every Man,
and an Excluſion of any religious Teſt for ever.

LONDON:

Printed by J. P. COGHLAN, No. 37, Duke-Street
Groſvenor-Square. 1790.

A SHORT ACCOUNT

OF THE

ESTABLISHMENT

OF THE

NEW SEE OF BALTIMORE.

T H E Roman Catholic religion was introduced into Maryland, together with the firſt ſetlers in the reign of Charles I. who granted that province to the Lord Baltimore a catholic nobleman, as a refuge for perſons of his religion from the ſeverity of the penal laws, which that unfortunate monarch wanted either the power or the fortitude to reſtrain. A number of catholic gentlemen and others emigrated from England and Ireland with the hope of enjoying that repoſe in the new ſettlement, which was denied them in their native country. The unrelenting ſpirit of per-

B   ſecution

lecution purfued them over the Atlantic. It deprived them of the juft fruits of their labours, it debarred them from every poft of truft and profit in the colony which they had fettled, it compelled them to maintain Proteftant minifters, and finally it enforced againft them many of the Britifh penal laws, from the cruelty of which they had fled. R. F. Andrew White an Englifh Jefuit of eminent piety and zeal accompanied the firft colonifts in 1632, and from that date till the late revolution the American catholics in Maryland and Virginia were conftantly ferved by Jefuit miffioners fucceffively fent from England. About the year 1720 the R. F. Grayton and others introduced catholicity into Penfylvania, and it has fince received a remarkable increafe in that province. Since the peace of 1783 and the fettlement of the American conftitution, penal laws are no longer known, and Catholics enjoy an equal participation of the rights of human nature with their neighbours of every other religious denomination. The very term of *toleration* is exploded, becaufe it imports a power in one predominant feft to indulge that religious liberty to others, which all claim as an inherent right. Catholic clergymen of various orders and nations

tions have reforted to America, and they every where find an ample vineyard to cultivate. In this ftate of religious freedom the clergymen judged it expedient to give ftability and dignity to the catholic religion by the eftablifh- ment of a regular hierarchy, and they therefore petitioned from the Pope the creation of an epifcopal See and the appointment of a diocefan Bifhop. The Pope applauding their zeal gracioufly admitted their requeft, and allowed them to elect their firft Bifhop. The Rev. Dr. John Carroll who had been for fome years the fuperior of the miffion was the object of their choice, and this Gentleman was accordingly appointed firft Bifhop of Baltimore. Upon the receipt of his Bulls from Rome he immediately repaired to England where his perfon and merit were well known, and prefented himfelf for confecration to the Right Rev. Dr. Charles Walmefley Bifhop of Rama, fenior Vicar Apoftolical of the catholic religion in this kingdom. By invitation of Thomas Weld Efq. the confe- cration of the new Bifhop was performed during a folemn high Mafs in the elegant chapel at Lulworth Caftle, on Sunday the 15th day of

of Auguſt 1790, being the feaſt of the Aſſumption of the Bleſſed Virgin Mary, and the mu-
nificence of that gentleman omitted no cir-
cumſtance which could poſſibly add dignity
to ſo venerable a ceremony. The two Prelates were attended by their reſpective aſſiſtant
prieſts and acolytes according to the rubric
of the Roman Pontifical; the richneſs of their
veſtments, the muſic of the choir, the multi-
tude of wax lights and the ornaments of the
altar concurred to increaſe the ſplendor of
the ſolemnity, which made a laſting impreſſion
upon every beholder. When the whole com-
pany was ſeated, the following ſhort addreſs
was delivered to the congregation by one of
the aſſiſtant Prieſts.

A SHORT

.

A SHORT ADRESS,

DELIVERED AUGUST 15, 1790.

IN THE

CHAPEL OF LULWORTH CASTLE,

AT THE CONSECRATION

OF THE RIGHT REVEREND

Dr. JOHN CARROLL,

APPOINTED FIRST BISHOP OF THE NEW
ERECTED SEE OF BALTIMORE IN NORTH
AMERICA.

✠

OUR bleſſed Lord and Redeemer hav-
ing defeated the powers of hell by the triumph
of the croſs, formed to himſelf a kingdom on
earth which was to conſiſt of the choſen of
every nation, becauſe all nations were now
become his own by right of conqueſt. The
Sun of juſtice which roſe from the Eaſt, has
in its progreſs enlightened every region of the
globe, and the kingdom of Chriſt, the church,
under the government of his Vicar and of
paſtors

pastors deputed by him, has successively embraced the whole world. Ages succeed ages, empires subvert empires, but the empire of Jesus Christ perseveres ever one and the same, ever persecuted and ever conquering, because all human revolutions are entirely subservient to it, and the formation of the kingdom of Christ is the ultimate object of the whole dispensation of providence in the government of this world. Never perhaps was this truth more sensibly evinced, than in the late violent convulsions, by which the hand of the Almighty has dismembered the great British empire, and has called forth into existence a new empire in the Western world, the destinies of which, we trust, are founded in his tenderest mercies. For although this great event may appear to us to have been the work, the sport of human passions, yet the earliest and most precious fruit of it has been the extension of the kingdom of Christ, the propagation of catholic religion, which heretofore fettered by restraining laws, is now enlarged from bondage and is left at liberty to exert the full energy of divine truth. Already is catholicity extended to the utmost boundaries of the immense continent of America, thousands are there earnestly demanding catholic instructors,

and

and all penetrated with reverence for the apoftolical See of St. Peter have concurred to
demand, from his fucceffor a catholic prelate,
whofe knowledge and whofe zeal may eftablifh
the faith of Peter upon the ruins of thofe er-
rors, which the firft inhabitants carried forth
with them from this country. But if Britain
infeɛted them with error, we have the confola-
tion to know that their catholicity is alfo derived immediately from us; and as we in for-
mer ages received the faith of Rome from the
great St. Gregory and our apoftle St. Auftin,
fo now at the interval of twelve hundred years,
our venerable prelate the heir of the virtues
and labours of our apoftle, will, this day, by
commiffion from the fucceffor of St. Gregory,
confecrate the firft Father and Bifhop of the
new church, deftined, as we confide, to inhe-
rit thofe benediɛtions which the firft called
have ungratefully rejeɛted. Glorious is this
day, my brethren, for the church of God
which fees new nations crouding into her bo-
fom; glorious for the prelate eleɛt, who goes
forth to conquer thefe nations for Jefus Chrift,
not by the efforts of human power, but in the
might of thofe weapons which have ever tri-
umphed in this divine warfare; he is not
armed with the ftrength of this world, but he
is

is powerful in piety, powerful in zeal, powerful
in evangelical poverty and firm reliance on
the protection of that God who sends him.
Glorious is this event, for his numerous spiri-
tual children, to whom his virtues have long
endeared him, comforting it is to us who have
been long connected with him by the virtu-
ous ties of education profession and friendship;
but in a special manner, my brethren, honou-
rable and comforting is this awful solemnity
to his and our common benefactor, the founder of this holy sanctuary, which shall be re-
vered through succeeding ages, even by churches yet un-named, as the privileged, the hap-
py spot, from whence their episcopacy and
hierarchy took their immediate rise; and this
precious distinction will be justly attributed to
the protection and favour of the glorious mother of God, whose house it is*, and through
whose patronage all christian churches are
founded. On this her greatest solemnity, my
brethren, it is your duty to implore the particular assistance of the great Queen of heaven;
and while you are edified by the solemn rites
with which the Catholic Church consecrates
her prelates, you will earnestly sollicit the

* It is dedicated to the B. V. Mary.

descent

defcent of the Holy Ghoft on the Bifhop eleft, that·like another Auftin he may worthily fulfil the extent of the apoftlefhip to which he is called, and when you implore for him the fevenfold grace of the Holy Spirit, you will not fail to demand it through the interceffiqn of her whom you daily falute, " Mother of divine grace."

In full confidence of her proteftion and blefling upon our miniftry, we proceed to the folemnity of the Confecration.

THE AUTHORITY

OF HIS HOLINESS

P O P E   P I U S   VI.

FOR CONSTITUTING THE

𝕹𝕖𝖜 𝕾𝖊𝖊 𝖔𝖋 𝕭𝖆𝖑𝖙𝖎𝖒𝖔𝖗𝖊 𝖎𝖓 𝔐𝖆𝖗𝖞𝖑𝖆𝖓𝖉.

TRANSLATED FROM THE ORIGINAL.

FOR THE REMEMBRANCE OF POSTERITY.

W H E N from the eminence of our apo-
ſtolical ſtation, we bend our attention to the
different regions of the earth, in order to fulfil to the utmoſt extent of our power the duty
which our Lord has impoſed upon our unwor-
thineſs of ruling and feeding his flock; our
care and ſolicitude are particularly engaged,
that the Faithful of Chriſt who diſperſed
through various provinces are united with us
by Catholic communion, may be governed by
their proper paſtors and diligently inſtructed
by them in the diſcipline of evangelical life
and doctrine.   For it is our principle, that they
who relying on the divine aſſiſtance have re-
gulated their lives and manners, agreeably to
· the

the precepts of Chriftian wifdom, ought fo to
command their own paffions as to promote by
the purfuit of juftice their own and their
neighbour's fpiritual advantage; and that they,
who have received from their Bifhops, and by
checking the intemperance of felf-wifdom,
have fteadily adhered to the heavenly doctrine
delivered by Chrift to the Catholic Church,
fhould not be carried away by every wind of
doctrine, but grounded on the authority of
divine revelation fhould reject the new and
varying doctrines of men, which endanger the
tranquility of government, and reft in the un-
changeable faith of the Catholic Church. For
in the prefent degeneracy of corrupt manners
into which human nature ever refifting the
fweet yoke of Chrift is hurried, and in the
pride of talents and knowledge which difdains
to fubmit the opinions and dreams of men to
the evangelical truth delivered by Jefus Chrift,
fupport muft be given by that heavenly authority which is entrufted to the Catholic Church
as to a fteady pillar and folid foundation which
fhall never fail, that from her voice and in-
ftructions mankind may learn the objects of
their faith and the rules of their conduct, not
only for the obtaining of eternal falvation, but
alfo for the regulation of this life and the

main-

maintaining of concord in the fociety of this
earthly city. Now this charge of teaching
and ruling firft given to the apoftles and efpecially to St. Peter the prince of the apoftles,
on whom alone the church is built, and to
whom our Lord and Redeemer entrufted the
feeding of his lambs and of his fheep, has been
derived in due order of fucceffion to Bifhops,
and efpecially to the Roman Pontiffs, fucceffors of St. Peter and heirs of his power and
dignity, that thereby it might be made evident that the gates of hell can never prevail
againft the church, and that the divine founder
of it will ever affift it to the confummation of
ages, fo that neither in the depravity of morals nor in the fluctuation of novel opinions
the epifcopal fucceffion fhall ever fail or the
bark of Peter be funk. Wherefore it having
reached our ears that in the flourifhing com-
monwealth of the Thirteen American States
many faithful Chriftians united in communion
with the chair of Peter, in which the centre
of catholic unity is fixed, and governed in
their fpiritual concerns by their own priefts
having care of fouls, earneftly defire that a
Bifhop may be appointed over them to exercife the functions of epifcopal order, to feed
them more largely with the food of falutary
doctrine,

doctrine, and to guard more carefully that portion of the catholic flock; We willingly embraced this opportunity which the grace of Almighty God has afforded us to provide thofe diftant regions with the comfort and miniftry of a Catholic Bifhop. And that this be effected more fuccefsfully and according to the rules of the facred canons, We commiflioned our Venerable brethren the Cardinals of the holy Roman church, directors of the Congregation *de propaganda fide*, to manage this bufinefs with the greateft care, and to make a report to us. It was therefore appointed by their decree, approved by us, and publifhed the twelfth day of July of the laft year, that the priefts who lawfully exereife the facred miniftry and have care of fouls in the united States of Ameiica, fhould be empowered to advife together and to determine, firft, in what town the epifcopal See ought to be erected, and next who of the aforefaid priefts appeared the moft worthy and proper to be promoted to this important charge, whom We, for this firft time only, and by fpecial grace permitted the faid priefts to elect and to prefent to this apoftolical See. In obedience to this decree the aforefaid priefts exercifing the cure of fouls in the United States of America, unanimoufly

unanimoufly agreed, that a Bifhop with ordinary jurifdiction ought to be eftablifhed in the
town of Baltimore, becaufe this town fituate in
Maryland which province the greater part of
the priefts and of the faithful inhabit, appeared the moft conveniently placed for inter-
courfe with the other States, and becaufe
from this province Catholic religion and faith
had been propagated into the others. And
at the time appointed for the election, they
being affembled together, the facrifice of holy
Mafs being celebrated, and the grace and
affiftance of the Holy Ghoft being implored,
the votes of all prefent were taken, and of
twenty fix priefts who were affembled twenty
four gave their votes for our beloved fon
John Carroll, whom they judged the moft proper to fupport the burden of epifcopacy, and
fent an authentic inftrument of the whole
tranfaction to the aforefaid Congregation of
Cardinals. Now all things being maturely
weighed and confidered in this Congregation,
it was eafily agreed that the interefts and increafe of Catholic religion would be greatly
promoted, if an epifcopal See were erected at
Baltimore, and the faid John Carroll were appointed the Bifhop of it. We therefore, to
whom this opinion has been reported by our
beloved

beloved fon Cardinal Antonelli Prefect of the
faid Congregation, having nothing more at
heart than to enfure fuccefs to whatever tends
to the propagation of true religion and to the
honour and increafe of the Catholic Church;
by the plenitude of our apoftolical power, and
by the tenour of thefe prefent, do eftablifh
and erect the aforefaid town of Baltimore into
an epifcopal See for ever, for one Bifhop to be
chofen by us in all future vacancies; and We
therefore, by the apoftolical authority aforefaid, do allow, grant and permit to the Bifhop
of the faid city, and to his fucceffors in all future times, to exercife epifcopal power and jurifdiction, and to hold and enjoy all and every
right and privilege of order and jurifdiction,
and of every other epifcopal function, and
which Bifhops conftituted in other places are
empowered to hold and enjoy in their refpective churches, cities and diocefes, by right,
cuftom or by other means, by general privi-
leges, graces, indults and apoftolical difpenfa-
tions, together with all pre-eminencies, ho-
nours, immunities, graces and favours, which
other Cathedral Churches, by right or cuftom, or in any other fort, have, hold and enjoy. We moreover decree and declare the
faid epifcopal See thus erected, to be fubject
or

or fuffragan to no Metropolitan right or jurifdiction, but to be for ever fubject immediately to us, and to our fucceffors the Roman
pontiffs, and to this apoftolical See. And till
another opportunity fhall be prefented to us
of eftablifhing other Catholic Bifhops in the
United States of America, and till other dif-
pofitions fhall be made by this apoftolical See,
We declare, by our apoftolical authority, all
the Faithful of Chrift living in Catholic communion, as well ecclefiaftics as feculars, and
all the clergy and people dwelling in the aforefaid United States of America, though hither-
to they may have been fubject to other Bifhops
of other diocefes, to be henceforward fubject
to the Bifhop of Baltimore in all future times;
and to this Bifhop and to his fucceffors we
impart power to curb and check, without ap-
peal, all perfons who may contradict or op-
pofe their orders, to vifit perfonally or by de-
puties all Catholic Churches, to remove abu-
fes, to correct the manners of the faithful,
and to perform all things which other Bifhops
in their refpective diocefes are accuftomed to
do and perform, faving in all things our own
authority and that of this apoftolical See.
And, whereas by fpecial grant, and for this
firft

firft time only, we have allowed the priefts exercifing the cure of fouls in the United States of America, to elect a perfon to be appointed Bifhop by us, and almoft all their votes have been given to our beloved fon John Carroll Prieft; We being otherwife certified of his faith, prudence, piety and zeal, forafmuch as by our mandate he hath during the late years directed the fpiritual government of fouls, do therefore, by the plenitude of our authority, declare, create, appoint and conftitute the faid John Carrol Bifhop and Paftor of the faid church of Baltimore, granting to him the faculty of receiving the rite of confecration from any Catholic Bifhop holding communion with the apoftolical See, affifted by two Ecclefiaftics vefted with fome dignity, in cafe that two Bifhops cannot be had, firft having taken the ufual oath according to the Roman Pontifical. And we commiffion the faid Bifhop elect to erect a church in the faid city of Baltimore, in form of a Cathedral Church, inafmuch as the times and circumftances may allow, to inftitute a body of clergy deputed to divine worfhip and to the fervice of the faid church, and moreover to eftablifh an epifcopal feminary either in the fame city

D   or

or elfewhere as he fhall judge moft expedient,
to adminifter ecclefiaftical incomes, and to
execute all other things which he fhall think
in the Lord to be expedient for the increafe
of Catholic faith and the augmentation of the
worfhip and fplendour of the new-erected
church. We moreover enjoin the faid Bifhop
to obey the injunctions of our Venerable
brethren the Cardinals Directors of the facred Congregation *de propaganda fide*, to
tranfmit to them at proper times a relation of
his vifitation of his church, and to inform
them of all things which he fhall judge to be
ufeful to the fpiritual good and falvation of
the flock trufted to his charge. We therefore decree that thefe our letters are and ever
fhall be firm, valid and efficacious, and fhall
obtain their full and entire effect, and be
obferved inviolable by all perfons whom it
now doth or hereafter may concern; and that
all Judges ordinary and delegated, even audi-
tors of caufes of the facred apoftolical palace,
and Cardinals of the holy Roman church
muft thus judge and define, depriving all
and each of them of all power and authority to judge or interpret in any other manner,
and declaring all to be null and void, if any
one,

one, by any authority, fhould prefume, either knowingly or unknowingly, to attempt any thing contrary thereunto. Notwithftanding all apoftolical, general or fpecial conftitutions and ordinations, publifhed in univerfal, provincial and fynodical councils, and all things contrary whatfoever.

Given at Rome at St. Mary Major, under the Fifherman's Ring (Seal) the 6th day of November 1789, and in the 15th Year of our Pontificate.

D U P L I C A T E.

L. S.

R. CARD. BRASCHI ONESTI.

NOTES

––––––

The preceding pages, copied in fac-simile, by photo-lithographic process, for the HISTORICAL CLUB, from a very rare pamphlet secured in England by the Rev. Francis L Hawks, D. D., LL. D., and now in the possession of the Rev. Wm. Stevens Perry, D. D., shew that, in marked contrast with the care taken that, at the Consecration of Seabury, and of White and Provoost, all should be done in accordance with the ancient Canons, the Romish hierarchy in this country began with a most irregular consecration, by *one* Bishop—a Bishop " *in partibus*," and this, as will be seen, authorized by a Papal Bull.

––––––

Pages 20 to 32 of the pamphlet herewith reprinted, are taken up with " Extracts from the different Bills of Right and Constitutions of the Thirteen United States of North America : declaring Liberty of Conscience as the Birth-

right of all men. With copies of their Oaths
of Allegiance and Trust."

It seems sufficient here, without reprinting
these Extracts in full, to cite their Headings.
which are, *verbatim et literatim*, as follows:

New Hampshire Bill of Rights,—Part I. Article 5.
Dated at Concord, Oct. 31, 1783.

Massachusets Constitution, Part I. Article 2.   *Dated
at Cambridge, March* 2. 1780.

Rhode Island Charter;—14th Charles II.

*Connecticut signed the General Convention, esteeming
any particular Declaration unnecessary.*

New York Constitution, April 20, 1777.—*Articles*
38. *and* 39.

New Jersey Constitution,—July 2, 1776.—*Art.* 18.

Pensylvania Declaration of Rights,—Sept. 28, 1776.
—*Chap.* 1. *Art.* 2.—*Chap.* 2. *Sect.* 10.—*Sect.* 40.

Delaware Declaration of Rights,—Sept. 20, 1776—
Sect. 2. *and* 3.—*Constitution, Art.* 22.

Maryland Declaration of Rights,—Aug. 14. 1776.—
Art. 33. 35.—*Constitution, Art.* 55.

Virginia signed the General Convention.

North Carolina—Dec. 19. 1776.—*Declaration of
Rights, Art.* 19.—*Constitution, Art.* 34. 40. 41.

South Carolina signed the Convention.

Georgia Constitution—Feb. 5. 1777.—*Art.* 56.

EXTRACTS from the GENERAL CONSTITU-
TIONAL DECLARATIONS of the THIRTEEN
UNITED STATES of AMERICA, assembled in
CONGRESS, September 17. 1787, and the 12th
of their INDEPENDENCE.

It is curious to notice the evident satisfaction
these Declarations as to liberty of conscience
gave to English and American Romanists in
1790, and then read the *Encyclicals* of Gregory
XVI, (August 13, 1832), and of Pius IX, (De-
cember 8, 1863), denouncing the "insanity" *
of those who declare, that, "Liberty of conscience is the right of every man, and that this
right ought in every well governed State to be
proclaimed and asserted by the law," † and the
79th Article of the *Syllabus*, stigmatizing the
error of those who deny "That the civil liberty
of every mode of worship, and, the full power
given to all of overtly and publicly manifesting
their opinions, and their ideas, of all kinds
whatsoever, conduce more easily to corrupt the
morals and minds of the people, and to the
propagation of the pest of indifferentism.‡

---

* "Deliramentum."

† "Libertatem conscientiae et cultuum, esse proprium cujus-
cumque hominis jus, quod lege proclamari et asseri debet in
omni recte constitutâ societate."

‡ "Civilem cujusque cultus libertatem, itemque plenam potes-
tatem omnibus attributam quaslibet opiniones cogitationesque
palam publiceque manifestandi, conducere ad populorum mores
animosque facilius corrumpendas, ac indifferentismi pestem
propagandam."

www.ingramcontent.com/pod-product-compliance
Lightning Source LLC
Chambersburg PA
CBHW021459090426
42739CB00009B/1791